Cute Christmas Coloring Book

ColorFun
PUBLISHING

Please help to leave your review about
this book.
With your feedback, we'll make
our next books even better!

Thanks, and enjoy your coloring
journey.

This Book Belongs to

"My idea of Christmas, whether old-fashioned or modern, is very simple: loving others." —Bob Hope

Helpful Tips for Coloring

Experiment different tools for coloring: crayons, colored pencils, markers, fine tip pens, pastels, etc. You can even mix different tools on images to see what works best for you. **Remember the spirit: Have Fun!**

Before you start, test your tool on the coloring test page. This little move will make sure a great start on your coloring work.

When using colored pencils, make sure they are sharp so that you can cover small areas or fine details with ease.

When using colored pencils, crayons or pastels, **start out light!** You can always go back and darken your colors.

Follow your instinct! You can start on any image of your choice and pick up any color you feel like at that particular moment for your coloring work. Make sure it's a precious process that allows inner talk!

Perfection is NOT the goal! Enjoy coloring and let your creativity go wild. After finishingn this coloring book, go back and see how your creativity has evolved over the images.

HAVE A GREAT TIME COLORING!

Color Test Page

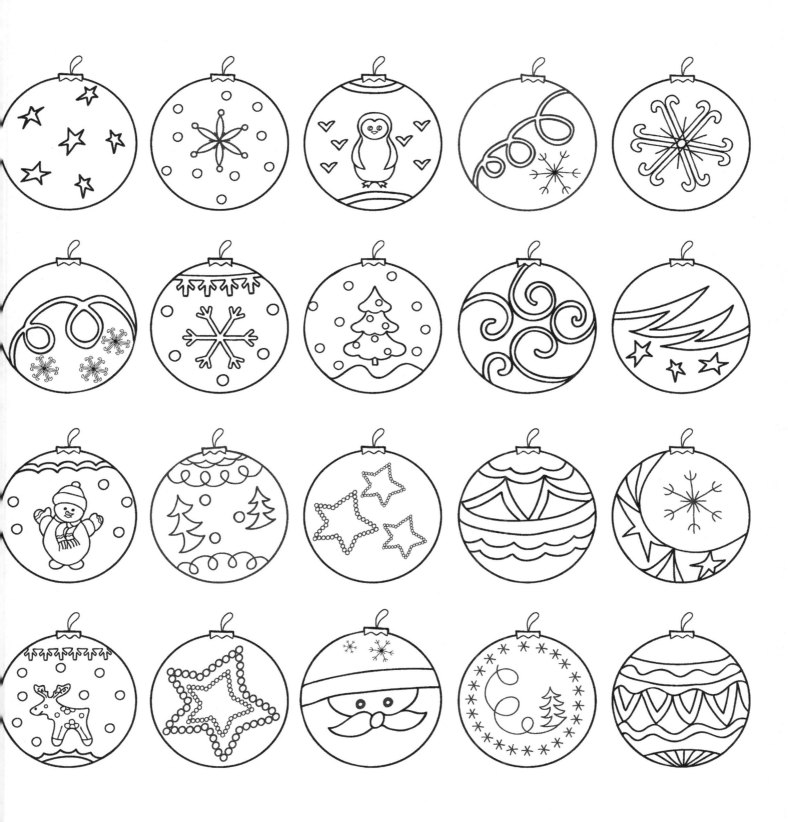

Christmas is about sharing
and
sharing is loving!

Christmas is about sharing
and
sharing is loving!

Christmas is about sharing
and
sharing is loving!

Christmas is about sharing
and
sharing is loving!

Christmas is about sharing
and
sharing is loving!

Christmas is about sharing
and
sharing is loving!

Christmas is about sharing
and
sharing is loving!

Christmas is about sharing
and
sharing is loving!

Christmas is about sharing
and
sharing is loving!

Christmas is about sharing
and
sharing is loving!

Christmas is about sharing
and
sharing is loving!

Christmas is about sharing
and
sharing is loving!

Christmas is about sharing
and
sharing is loving!

Christmas is about sharing
and
sharing is loving!

Christmas is about sharing
and
sharing is loving!

Christmas is about sharing
and
sharing is loving!

Christmas is about sharing
and
sharing is loving!

Christmas is about sharing
and
sharing is loving!

Christmas is about sharing
and
sharing is loving!

Christmas is about sharing
and
sharing is loving!

Christmas is about sharing
and
sharing is loving!

Christmas is about sharing
and
sharing is loving!

Christmas is about sharing
and
sharing is loving!

Christmas is about sharing
and
sharing is loving!

Christmas is about sharing
and
sharing is loving!

Christmas is about sharing
and
sharing is loving!

Christmas is about sharing
and
sharing is loving!

Christmas is about sharing
and
sharing is loving!

Christmas is about sharing
and
sharing is loving!

Christmas is about sharing
and
sharing is loving!

Christmas is about sharing
and
sharing is loving!

Christmas is about sharing
and
sharing is loving!

Christmas is about sharing
and
sharing is loving!

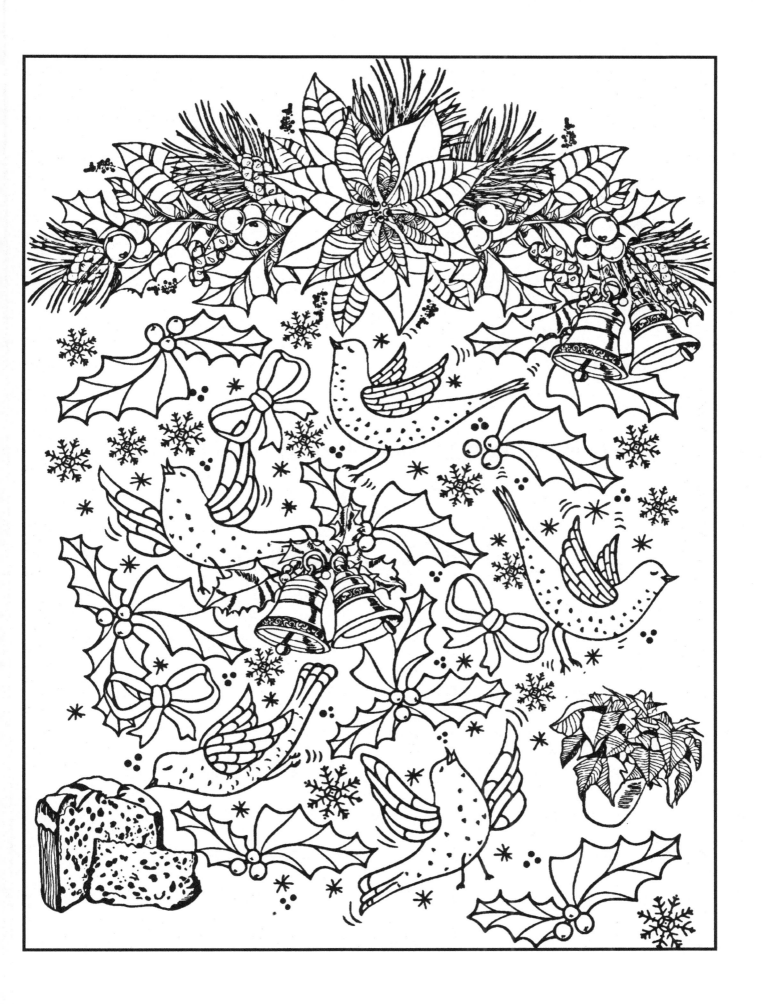

Christmas is about sharing
and
sharing is loving!

Christmas is about sharing
and
sharing is loving!

Christmas is about sharing
and
sharing is loving!

Merry Christmas !

Christmas is about sharing
and
sharing is loving!

Christmas is about sharing
and
sharing is loving!

Christmas is about sharing
and
sharing is loving!

Christmas is about sharing
and
sharing is loving!

Christmas is about sharing
and
sharing is loving!

Christmas is about sharing
and
sharing is loving!

Christmas is about sharing
and
sharing is loving!

Christmas is about sharing
and
sharing is loving!

Christmas is about sharing
and
sharing is loving!

Christmas is about sharing

and

sharing is loving!

Christmas is about sharing
and
sharing is loving!

Christmas is about sharing
and
sharing is loving!

Christmas is about sharing
and
sharing is loving!

Congratulations!
You've completed your
coloring journey!

Visit below link for free digital download version:
https://colokara.com/cutexmas